How To Read People And Spot A Liar

----- ✧✦✧ -----

Never be Lied to Again

Table of Contents

Can You Learn To Spot a Liar?..1

Why Training on How to Spot a Liar Is the Most Important Tool in Your Life 3

Psychology of Lying 5

How Important to You is Truth?..13

How Good Are You at Detecting Lies and Deceit?.................. 19

Lie Detection Techniques 23

Eye Movement Lying Signs - 11 Tips to Spot a Liar 25

Body Language: 8 Quick Tips on Learning How to Spot a Liar 27

Intuition Helps You Detect Dishonesty 29

Escaping the Power of Lies..31

Debunking the Common Myths about Liars.......................... 39

Application in Relationships: 10 Signs That She is Lying to You 41

Application to Personal Life 45

How to Tell if Someone is Lying in a Job Interview in Less Than One Minute 49

The One Dead Giveaway Almost Every Liar Makes When Telling a Story 53

Find Out if Anyone is on Drugs in Less Than Three Minutes 57

Find Out Who's Stealing and Whom You Can Trust 61

Is The Wool Being Pulled Over Your Eyes in a Negotiation? Find Out 69

How to Get Someone to Confess When You Have No Leverage Whatsoever 73

How to Tell Anyone's True Intent in Any Situation by Asking Four Simple Questions 77

BONUS 83

How to Use Hypnotic Suggestions Like a Pro in Only Minutes 83

Conclusion 95

Can You Learn To Spot a Liar?

Can you really LEARN to tell if someone is lying? Is this a trainable attribute that you may improve over time, so you can become a human lie detector? Or are some people just naturally proficient at detecting liars, while others might be more prone to accept lies without being able to determine untruths for what they are? If you feel you are the easily taken advantage of, then you might be wondering if you just have to find that skill, or discover the secrets and techniques to spot untrustworthy people. Is this an inbuilt talent - or learned skill - or both?

The answer to this is that it truly is a bit of both - but mainly it is not talent, but learning the skills. Talent is an innate ability to be able to do something. Yet people with talent need to learn more, they might just be faster learners than those who might not seem to be as inherently talented. This sometimes means that the talented are not as motivated, and imagine their natural abilities don't need to be improved by further training which is a waste of incredible promise.

So, in the end, it doesn't really matter if you happen to have a respectable knack to read peoples true intentions. You still need to learn and investigate the intricate details of spotting liars - so everyone will be able to get this skill in the end!

So, what do we need to do to understand how to tell if someone is lying?

Here are some tips you should know when embarking on increasing your lie detecting abilities.

Learning is doing. So, while studying and researching are necessary to get the understanding of what you should do, there is not much else that embeds education like DOING. Training what you learn is critical. Actually thinking about the tips you might have read and applied it with real thought is the foundation of skill development. Don't think you can just read!

Repeating, that is just doing it a few times does not improve your abilities; you need to practice more and more. As an illustration, sports stars don't happen to be so amazing by training once in a while - they train hardcore and often.

Analysis - Just practice is not adequate though, as there will be a concluding capstone point which is an examination. You must think about what you are doing, the way you are doing it, what the outcomes were, plus methods to enhance it. Each time you go out trying to notice someone that is lying, you need to debrief afterward and think about what worked and what didn't. This consideration period is essential to embedding information and improving your skills at detecting if someone is lying to you.

So, keep these in mind as you learn how to tell if someone is lying to you. Practice makes perfect, no matter how naturally talented you are!

You Can Do This

Why Training on How to Spot a Liar Is the Most Important Tool in Your Life

Although statistics vary, it is evident we communicate more with our nonverbal behaviours, than we do with the words we use. This means, having the ability to read the real hidden emotions of people could put a whole new twist on the lie detection.

When a group of students trained on how to spot a liar was asked only to read a criminal's nonverbal behaviour, they were over 70% accurate. This is well above standard as we are only better than chance at detecting a lie. How to tell when someone is lying is very hard, especially if you're unaware of the possible signs. Can you actually learn what and how to spot signs of hidden emotions that could ultimately lead to lies?

You can not only learn what to look for, but with practice, you can learn what questions can expose the lie further. But keep in mind, it is not about detecting lies, it is about identifying behaviours brought on by stress. For example, what if during a sales deal you were able to spot a behaviour opposite the words of the conversation. "That's my bottom line," may mean nothing if you spot a quick sign of contempt showing something different than the words. If trained to detect these behaviours, you would indeed protect your pocketbook by negotiating further.

Let's take a quick look at contempt. One side of the salesperson's mouth raised in a split second, indicating he may be hiding something. In this case, the seller knows it is not his bottom line. Can you imagine the impact this type of training can have on your life?

There may be times identifying a lie is not in your best interest, such as infidelity. Or is it? But what about a major sales deal where there are millions on the line. How about during the negotiation phase, you ask if what you are purchasing can be manufactured on time. Spotting a leak in emotion could mean millions in sales.

Training on how to spot a liar is incredibly overlooked, but possibly the most valuable asset in your business and personal life. But you get a lot more than how to identify hidden emotions, more importantly, it teaches you how your nonverbal behaviours can affect the conversation. Knowing what contempt looks like, you can use it to re-route a conversation to your way of thinking.

On any given day, someone will hear nearly 200 different lies. This is disturbing, but what is more concerning, are the lies that are meant to hurt you personally, or your career. Although you will not detect all lies as this is impossible, if trained, you may detect that one lie that could forever change your life.

Psychology of Lying

Psychology is a surprising and wonderful subject by means of which a person is enabled to study the minds of the individuals. It is an art as well as a science. It is an art in the sense that everything concerned with the individual is defined clearly and discussed elaborately. It is a science in the sense that there are experiments conducted in studying the characteristics and behavioural activities of the persons with individual difference. Using the knowledge of psychology, an expert knows how to spot a liar using some special methods.

How to tell if someone is lying?

One of the signs of lying is detected by frequent use of promising words like "I am honestly telling you the truth". Some people behave in an extraordinary way to hide their inefficiency to achieve their goals in certain things, and choose to lie as an alternative weapon. An expert in criminal psychology finds a clue to tell if someone is lying by analyzing the individual's indifferent behaviour and over promising words. Asking relevant questions to the person suspected is a good technique to detect a liar. From the facial expression and likely fumbling words, the lying can be confirmed. Also there are the poligraph machines to measure the psychological stress detection from the facial expressions and cadenced speech.

Types of lying:

Basically lying can be classified into three ways and explain why people lie.

- a) Habitual lying: Some people are used to telling lies as a habit, whether good or bad. It is purely a habit of lying for nothing. It's often not being done for any type of gain. It is difficult to make the person who does it all the time, to realize that it is not goodtrait..
- b) Compulsive lying: In a few cases people are compelled to tell lies, the compulsion being out of a self-based need or an external force. Such type of lying is known as compulsive lying.
- c) Delusive lying: This type of lying is of worst nature because it is harmful to others. It is highly deceptive in its consequences, with the utmost bad intention of cheating others and avoiding punishment.

Characteristics of lying:

There is one question to ask "Where are the liars?" The answer to this question is very simple, but really surprising, which may not seem believable. The suspense lies in the fact that liars are everywhere in the society, irrespective of sex and age. There is a research report saying that any human is thrown into circumstances to tell a lie at least once in every three or four weeks, which is really interesting.

- Lying is avoided when in a face-to-face meeting.
- Liars choose the phone as the best channel for lying

- Lying is sometimes for fun and pleasure
- To hide one lie, subsequent lying can be seen with lying persons
- Sometimes lying is exaggerated for some hidden reasons
- Lying is in general harmful, but sometimes harmless

Is lying always bad?

There are two answers to this question. Whatever may be the answer, it should be justified for its strength. Lying is not a criminal act, even though it may be serious. If a person chooses to tell a lie for a better thing, it may be admitted in spite of its serious nature.

If the damage is caused with a bad intention to the good name of a person or a concern or a property, it cannot be borne with patience.

Alternatively, when a person comes forward to tell one or two lies in the interest of a genuine person in danger and genuine property at risk, it is admissible.

So, it is an undeniable fact that lying is not always harmful. It is only when it is for bad consequences with bad intention. Definitely, lying for good things is harmless. It is not punishable in view of the purpose behind it for a good thing.

Why Do Liars Lie?

Why do We Lie?

Mostly everyone, at some time, has lied. Come clean now: that incorporates you and me. Truth be told, a few people, dismal to say, lie constantly. Therapists call these individuals enthusiastic or psychopathic liars. They tell lies, notwithstanding when they don't need to. Indeed, even the most youthful of kids will lie, particularly on the off chance that they think by doing it they won't get rebuffed for something. At the point when kids first figure out how lying functions, they do not have the ethical comprehension of when to abstain from doing it.

Whilst everyone lies, few see how ruinous it can be, the reason we do it, or how to stop it.

So we should answer the inquiry, "Why do individuals lie?"

Why does the world lie? This is an inquiry with numerous answers.

Dread - It was Tad Williams (American fiction writer) who said, "We tell lies when we are anxious... perplexed of when we don't have the foggiest idea, apprehensive of what others will think, apprehensive of what will be gotten some answers concerning us. In any case, each time we tell a falsehood, the thing that we fear develops stronger."

People can be so perplexed of what may happen in the event that they came clean. Possibly they have accomplished something incorrectly and fear the outcomes of their activities, so they mislead and conceal what they did. As regularly said in regards to political outrages: It's not the wrongdoing that gets you in a bad position, more so the concealment.

Control - Lies are regularly persuaded by a craving to get other individuals to either accomplish something or not accomplish something, or to settle on a choice in the support of the individual doing the lying. Somebody may deceive to get something they are longing for. For example, sex, cash, status, power, love, and so forth.

Pride - Many times, a person will lie in light of pride. They utilize it to no end more than an apparatus to make a positive picture of themselves. This prompts misrepresentation, which is a type of lying. Frequently individuals will make interesting, yet totally false, stories about themselves to enhance their picture.

Lying may seem simple and harmless at first, but just like any addiction, you'll soon find yourself trapped and entangled more than you could have ever imagined.

The huge issue with lying is that it turns into a fixation. When you escape with a falsehood it regularly drives you to proceed with your duplicities, and all the while, we demolish connections, hurt others, lose our uprightness, and lose our peace. Truth turns into a dreaded foe of the liar. It's a wiped out and shocking cycle that doesn't ever have an upbeat completion.

Wouldn't you get a kick out of the chance to stay away from this cycle? You can settle on the decision at this moment to carry on with a legitimate life. I guarantee it is the better street... regardless of the possibility that you are perplexed. Here's the reason:

When you're straight, you can feel settled.

Lying is to a great degree unpleasant. It causes you to be always looking behind you and pondering who may discover you out. You're continually going through the falsehoods you've told in your mind, attempting to monitor what you've advised to which individual, and what's the following untruth you have to tell. When you're straightforward, you don't have those stresses or the negative results of your falsehoods.

Trustworthiness Builds Trust and Healthy Relationships

Individuals are always hoping to see who they can trust and who they can't. Individuals are very more discerning and mindful of who comes clean and who doesn't. After some time, genuineness shows itself as an attribute that is wonderful and profoundly regarded. As you live sans lie, you start to see individuals will trust and regard you to an ever increasing extent.

In the event that you oppose the enticement to lie, you increment your ability to fabricate enduring connections of trust. This is valid in every one of our connections whether it's dating, family, companions, or at work.

You like yourself and don't convey the weight of blame.

On the off chance that you are straightforward, it implies you do what you say you're going to do, and when you say something, individuals know you mean what you say, and that feels great. Somebody remarked about the estimation of being straightforward: "I used to lie a ton. I would lie simply because it was simpler than clarifying reality. Also, I have at long last developed to understand that it's less demanding to [be honest]. Being straightforward and open has really gotten me more than lying. My folks trust me, and I like myself. What's more, when you like yourself then you realize that all is well." This individual has come to understand that when we come clean and live it, we turn out to be candidly and profoundly more grounded each day.

Finally, you must learn how can you be a liar detective and I hope that this information will help you to get an idea of why we lie all the time.

How Important to You is Truth?

Rather than love, than money, than fame, give me the truth.
~Henry David Thoreau, Walden

Every time I read this quote from Thoreau, I get goose bumps. I agree with him completely. I don't know if there is any better feeling on earth than having an "aha" moment. It is that moment when a concept or idea solidifies in our mind and connects with all the other information we already have. Sometimes it is called a "eureka" moment.

If the truth shall set you free, then the lies can imprison you in guilt, burden, and regret. They come as small as the occasional white lies friends tell each other, to as big as the whopper of a lie governments tell their citizens. No matter the size, lies are intended to purposely deceive one into believing something, hide the truth or both. When we find out we've been lied to, we feel victimized. When it's been discovered that we've lied to, we feel like crawling under a rock. However, if you are on a pathway to improvement, you must give quality thought to the lies in your life.

Let's cover the following 5 categories of lies: Living a Lie, "Sensational-lie-zing", The Lies You Believe, The Lies You Tell, and Lying for a Good Cause,

Living a Lie

There is a woman who has successfully convinced every non-family member in her life that she is from another culture. She speaks the language, wears the clothes and when speaking English, mimics the accent to a tee. She didn't stop there though. Even though her family knows the truth of who she is and where she came from, she continues this charade in front of them as well. She has lived this lie for so long, that she convinced herself that it is true.

This woman takes living a lie to the extreme. However, there are those of us that may have created a new past for ourselves. We've made up memories and created experiences we've never had. We may have even replaced real memories with more pleasant memories to cover up a painful or resentment-filled experience.

When we live a lie, we are not living authentically. Instead of being the person we are, dealing with the choices we've made, and become better because of the experiences we've had, we push it deep down inside ourselves. We don't deal with it. Instead, we pretend until what we've made up feels real enough to treat it as such. What's interesting is that by dealing with a painful past, we can become more interesting than the life we've been living. By discovering our authentic self, we can feel free, have more fun, and care less about the judgment of others. This doesn't mean that you don't grow and change. It means that change occurs from the inside out so that you are always expressing the real you to the world.

How Important to You is Truth?

"Sensational-lie-zing"

People that sensationalize everything never heard the phrase, "if it sounds too good to be true, it probably is". Every interaction with them feels like they are selling you something, and the cost of what they are selling, is your belief in what they are saying. They have a flair for the dramatic, and in fact, personify the word itself. Their stories are a series of half-truths, exaggerations, and borrowed stories.

So what happens when someone disassembles one of their stories to call it out as a fraud? How do these folks deal with being discovered, to not have been telling the whole truth, or sometimes even a part of the truth? Often, they are willing to risk being found out for the reward of being the most interesting person in the room. They want to seem larger than life because they feel small inside. Their greatness comes from captivating a crowd's attention and imagination, and not through a belief in their own greatness.

It's difficult to find the real you interesting, if you are always hiding it. Rather than sensationalizing everything, bring it down a notch and let an interesting story stand on its own. Let the real you experience life. Be the giant you really are inside, rather than the giant you pretend to be. There is nothing like accepting yourself for who you really are.

The Lies You Believe

There are times when people may want to be deceived. The excitement of the moment overshadows reason, common sense, and intuition. When you want to believe something so much, it can be easy to suspend your disbelief. Picture the man or woman who says they are engaged to be married. However, the person they are engaged to is married, living with their spouse and kids. What happens when the engaged person realizes the truth of the situation? Usually, it's more heartache than they've ever imagined. Plus, they have the feeling that they allowed themselves to be deceived.

You don't have to believe a fairy tale to have to find excitement and happiness in life. The height of the feelings you experience in the fairy tale is equal only to the fall when the dream ends and reality sets back in again. There is a difference between optimism and fooling yourself. The difference between the two is remaining present, grounded, and centered.

The Lies You Tell

There was a story about an executive that blatantly lied during a meeting full of people. She made it seem as if a non-executive didn't do her job, while all along it was the executive who was the source of the problem all along. The non-executive was not allowed to reveal the truth about the executive out of fear of making her look bad in public, and the repercussions that would have in the future. However, it was clear that the executive was counting on that response. She never apologized and more than likely never lost sleep over what happened.

Here's the problem. That non-executive learned not to trust the executive. Therefore, she's going to document every conversation she and the executive has. So, the next time they are in a public forum and the lies begin, the non-executive will be prepared with emails, documents, schedules, and testimonials to counteract the lies that are sure to come.

How Important to You is Truth?

The first lesson here is when you tell lies, people catch on, predict your next move, and are prepared to 'out' you in public. The second lesson is that it can take one event to lose someone's trust and a very long time (if ever) to gain it back. The third lesson is that the more you lie, the easier it becomes to lie, and thus the more you lie. Lying becomes a self-sustaining cycle that can be hard to break. Don't start it. Take responsibility for your actions. It's easier and simpler than any one of the negative consequences one can experience from lying.

Lying For a Good Cause

Sometimes we may think it's better to lie than to tell the truth in order to spare someone's feelings. Whether the question deals with weight, looks, productivity, quality of work, or personality, we'll provide false compliments, grudgingly agree, or dodge the question completely. The issue is that our body language rarely lies. Therefore, our mouths are saying one thing while our body language contradicts us. Over 60% of our communication is body language while less than 10% is verbal (the words we speak). The rest of our communication is in tone (the way we speak).

When someone realizes that we aren't being truthful because our words and body language aren't in sync, they can become hurt. If they are asking for the truth, they can be especially hurt by the deception.

Instead, talk to them about the things you can sincerely compliment them on. Then, carefully provide constructive feedback on the areas where they may need a little assistance. In this way, you aren't criticizing them or focusing on the negative. You are complimenting what you can honestly compliment, and then building on that to mention areas where they can do even better.

Providing potentially hurtful feedback is never easy. However, lying to the person that asks for it may ultimately cause more hurt and damage than providing truthful feedback with a more positive spin.

How Good Are You at Detecting Lies and Deceit?

Some of us would describe ourselves as extremely gullible, falling for every trick, believing everything that is said to us. Others are more wary, often to the extent of believing nothing without proof and are extremely cynical.

In a broad sense, those who are gullible tend to be far more positive. They have a happier perspective and expect the best of everyone around them. They do not expect anyone to be deceitful or to lie to them. You may say that they see life through rose-tinted spectacles.

In contrast, the cynical person has a far more negative outlook, always looking for a catch or an underlying reason for someone being nice to them. They pride themselves on being able to detect lies or people who are trying to rip them off.

But when you really think about it, how easy is it to detect lies, or indeed, how easy is it to lie successfully? A poker player has to be good at lying; bluffing is a part of the game. But how do you know if a person is bluffing or just pretending to bluff? You may have seen Derren Brown (UK mindreader) when he taught a relatively elderly lady to play poker with the pros in just one week, demonstrating how easily one can learn to be a good bluffer and adept at reading others.

One must also be aware that anyone who has even a touch of social phobia will display all of the cues which may be confused as the indications of a lie. Many people, for example, are aware of their heart beating rapidly and their chest tightening when stopped by a police officer, even when they know they have done nothing wrong. At school, the majority of teenagers don't feel comfortable being asked to stand up and read aloud or to answer a question. They aren't lying; they are simply not comfortable in that situation.

There are many visible indicators of lies, such as sweating or avoiding eye contact, shuffling and so on. But if you know what the indicators are, you can learn to overcome them. I was with a group of people the other week discussing lie detection. There is no definitive test, no one indicator which you can truly rely upon. You cannot take anything alone, but have to look at the overall picture. You also have to recognize your own instinctive expectancies and learn to take a step back from them.

A person who expects to be lied to will have at least become practiced in the things which should be looked out for. But, and this is a big BUT, their own expectation will taint what they see; they are more inclined to see a lie, purely because they expect a lie, and because of this can misread the cues which are provided.

In reality, your expectations have a great impact on the reality which you subsequently experience. If you have a positive expectation you will notice the things which are positive in your life and the more negative events will be given less thought, less attention. Life will seem happier and better purely as a result of your expecting it to be better. You are also less likely to detect lies and deceit; you are not looking for it.

Those who are good at poker have learned how to step back from their emotions and to keep an open mind, always remaining observant as to the hidden cues which they are inevitably privy to, so long as they are looking for them. People do "give the game away" when they are trying to lie, although often this cue is only observable for a microsecond. What you observe may just be a fleeting glance of satisfaction, that micro-expression which tells you they feel good because they got one over on you.

Ask any poker player and they will say that there is far more satisfaction in winning off a poor hand than there is in winning off a good hand. The intrigue of bluffing and detecting bluffs is more what hooks the poker player, rather than just relying on being lucky enough to be dealt great cards.

Lie Detection Techniques

Profound lie detection techniques are hard to find. Throughout all my experiences I have learned lie detection techniques that I can utilize when I am under the impression that someone is lying. With these techniques, I can catch a liar almost every time. Here are the techniques:

1. While talking about a specific subject with a friend or any person, and their appearance is off or they are appearing to be deceptive, then here is what you do. You abruptly change the subject and making sure the subject is not pertinent to the subject the person appeared to be lying about. Now, vigilantly watch the person's face. A liar will become extremely relaxed and will welcome the change in subject. Watch their facial expressions carefully. A person who is not lying will have a puzzled look, and might even attempt to direct the conversation back to the previous one.

2. This technique is only effective when a person is telling a story. It has a very small margin of error when done correctly. Here is what you do. Allow the person to tell the entire story, and listen attentively for the sequence of events in the story. Now, ask him to do a full recount of the story, but this time backwards. You would need to have an extraordinary memory to restate a made up story backwards. Thus, if he can tell the story again

backwards, he is not lying. If he cannot, he is most likely lying. Try it yourself. Make up a story, and say it out loud. Now try repeating what you just said backwards. It is almost impossible. These techniques are all highly effective, and having the knowledge is extremely powerful. Once you learn these techniques, you will need to work on several things. You will need to time these techniques correctly, and you will need to know which lie detection technique to use in the situation

It is important to remember that the more you practice these techniques, the better you get at them. It is just like everything else, "practice makes perfect." The best advice I can give to aid you in catching liars using these techniques is that timing is pivotal.

Eye Movement Lying Signs - 11 Tips to Spot a Liar

If you suspect that someone you know is lying, there are specific things you can look out for. Eye movement lying and body language signs are some of the easiest to spot.

Here are 11 simple ways to spot a liar:

1. Avoid Eye Contact: A person who is lying often avoids eye contact. When asked a probing question, their eyes will usually look away. When flat out lying, people usually don't stare you in the eyes.

2. Rapid Eye Blinking: People who are lying also sometimes exhibit rapid blinking. When they get nervous, their eyes may start to blink more than normal.

3. Looking Up and To The Right: Another sign of eye movement lying is looking up and to the right.

4. Eyes Get Wider: Oftentimes, people's eyes become wider when lying. As they become nervous, their eyes may open more than normal.

5. Squinting Eyes: People also sometimes squint their eyes when lying.

6. Eye movement lying signs are not the only signs to look for, however. There are plenty of other body movements and facial expressions which show when a person is lying. Here are a few of the more common signs:

7. Nervousness

8. Sweating

9. Fidgeting

10. Voice becomes higher pitched

11. Body shifts positions

12. Voice pauses while talking

The last thing to note is to trust your gut. When you suspect that eye movement lying signs and body language is telling you one thing, you are probably right. Your intuition is usually right.

If you ever suspect that someone is lying to you, these are some extremely effective tips that will help you spot a liar within seconds. The techniques laid out in this guide are the same used effectively by law enforcement agencies, so they are extremely beneficial

Body Language: 8 Quick Tips on Learning How to Spot a Liar

Knowing how to spot a liar by their body language is one of many ways people catch on to deception. Most, if not all, of a liar's body language, comes from a conscious effort to perform regular unconscious actions. This includes breathing, limb movements, and eye movements, in addition to dead giveaways that no liar can control.

Here are 8 quick tips to catching a liar by observing their body language

- Liars might have a difficult time swallowing so they may clear their throat often

- Liars have a deep audible breath

- The emotional expressions of a liar are limited to the mouth region. When a liar smiles, crow's feet don't appear, the hallmark of an authentic smile.

- Liars tend to blink, A LOT

- Liars have a hard time looking you in the eye. [Beware, just because s/he doesn't make eye contact doesn't mean s/he is lying. The person might just be shy]

- Physical expression will be limited, with few arm and hand movements. what arm and hand movements are present will seem stiff, and mechanical. Hands, arm, and legs pull in toward the body; the individual takes up less space.

- Most hand contact will be limited to the face, neck, and shoulder areas. The mouth and ears are a particular hot spot.

- Liars force themselves to be relaxed and casual, so the control their body language. This leads to exaggerated movements, fake smiles (fake smiles don't exhibit crows feet around the eyes) or conversely they might just fold their arms or have their hands in their pockets to avoid all that.

Intuition Helps You Detect Dishonesty

Has anyone ever told you a sob story and you intuitively felt it wasn't true? Have you traveled to a city or town and intuitively knew its pristine reputation was built on quicksand? Read a magazine or newspaper article and intuitively smelled deceit? Heard about a job promotion and intuitively tasted rotten grapes? Whether you had similar or different experiences, you sense something is "false" when certain people communicate by 1) face-to-face or third party contact, 2) phone, fax or telegram, 3) letter, email or instant messaging, 4) Internet forum or blog, and 5) media broadcast or publication.

Your intuition senses dishonesty and the motive surrounding it. For example, in an email, Barbara tells her friend, Michael, about her crippling back injury suffered due to a taxi accident. After reading her email, he intuitively hears his inner voice say, "She fell stepping out of her bathtub. She lied to avert embarrassing herself and to receive more attention from her family and friends." He can confront her or let it go. The truth about her injury might be publicly revealed in a confession or by proof that could take months or years. Intuitively, Michael knows the truth.

Some people mastered the art of body language. For various situations, they look straight in your eyes, stand tall and give a firm handshake. They customize facial gestures and body poses. Some people mastered the art of spoken language. With crafted or ironed words, they perjure themselves, but several listeners will say, "They didn't mean it that way." Or, "They're genuine." Or, "They speak the truth." Such body and spoken languages might deceive your physical senses, but never your intuitive senses, even if you discount or ignore them. You possess an innate lie detector. When people are dishonest, notice if you intuitively see a vision of Pinocchio's growing nose, intuitively feel a distrustful feeling or intuitively hear the word, trickster. Perceive if you intuitively know a sham when it greets you. Discern if you intuitively smell an air of betrayal or intuitively say, "Pure fiction." You'll have these intuitive experiences or others.

When I encounter a dishonest person face-to-face, I intuitively see an inner vision pause in my mind's eye. The vision shows the truth, whether I accept or reject it. I recall an afternoon in which a woman I recently met invited me to a professional sports event. I asked her if she was married, before accepting her invitation. Without hesitation, she replied, "No." A paused vision showed the word, separated. She lied to get me to go out with her. I didn't confront her then because I had to rush to a business meeting. The next time we spoke, she admitted to being separated from her husband. "My intuition already told me," I informed her and ended our conversations. She was unavailable and marked untrustworthy.

Each day you're inundated with numerous types of communications from known and unknown people. Fabricated stories, cunning reputations, deceitful publications, phony promises and other dishonest acts won't fool you when you pay attention to your intuition.

Escaping the Power of Lies

Lying; obviously not a trait that one hopes for in a potential mate (A possible form of mistreatment in a relationship that can have you questioning your own sanity). Unfortunately, if in a relationship with a person who is incapable of being honest with you, their lies can take you on a terrible ride of emotional distress. Someone who is dishonest in their core being has the power of manipulating an unsuspecting victim, producing almost a brainwashing type effect and ultimately leaving them questioning their own abilities to judge right from wrong.

There is no clear-cut way of establishing why a person may be a chronic liar. Everyone is so very different, the reasons can range from the treatment they received as a child that has carried over into adulthood and can extend into the confusing and baffling case of a person lying for no logical reason. Perhaps the person's purpose was an attempt to obtain something from you, something you would not offer, had you known the truth. A person may simply be dishonest, selfish and unworthy of your love and their lying is an attempt to hold together a relationship that would not stand if honesty was only an acceptable choice. In the case of escaping the emotional hell of what this type of person is capable of doing to you, it does not matter why they are lying.

Do not waste any of your precious time trying to find reason in their unreasonable world. You most probably will never find the answers you seek. The answers hide within the person who is lying to you, and this most certainly will not be a source from which you will obtain any rational knowledge. Once accepting that fact, truly acknowledging this, you must let the urge to know "why" leave and you must replace it with the next step. It is of importance to understand what happens to the emotional state of a person who is the victim of a manipulative liar.

If you feel you may be in a relationship in which the other person is strongly misleading you, it is important to understand what is happening. You may be at the point that you are questioning your own judgment and you are not sure if you are paranoid or if you are the victim of lies. A calculating person can have you confused, bewildered and unable to see the relationship for what it truly is.

Lying is a demon that usually sneaks up slowly. All liars must begin with one initial lie. This is the starting point; that crucial moment when the person lying will learn if they can get away with it. It may start as a small lie, perhaps something inconsequential, that does not have a severe impact on the relationship. You are in love, so you are not questioning the other person's motives or words. Your feelings of love cause you to casually accept what the other person is saying to you. After all, they have not yet given you a reason to question them. Not yet, being the key words.

Once a chronic liar has placed their first lie, this is the first domino in their game. In their mind, this initial lie is part of the cement that will hold all the other lies. Having a small lie received with no difficulty gives the offender the belief that they are clever and cunning enough to try again. The victim has unknowingly stepped into the trap.

The second lie, third lie and perhaps fourth lie will be a bit larger than the initial one. These lies can range from an excuse as to why they did not call when they promised and extending to lies of their whereabouts. It may be at this point that things do not seem "quite right" to you. You may feel a twinge of suspicion, however, when in a serious relationship, you feel it is inappropriate to rush to a wrong conclusion. The lies have now been placed onto the cement foundation.

When the other person is playing an emotional game and their lies are the basis for obtaining whatever illogical goal they have, the lies will be told more rapidly and larger as the weeks and months move on. Unfortunately, the victim, already believing the initial lies, has given the perpetrator a belief of superiority and control. It is sad, indeed, when one person is giving out love and the other is giving out deceit. Time has moved on, the relationship appears stronger in the victim's eyes and unfortunately, the game does not quite end here.

At this point, the victim may begin to make inquiries. When being lied to, even by the most cunning of liars, one most certainly will eventually have the feeling that something is wrong. Maybe not in full awareness of exactly what is out of place; one will know that the words of the other person do not always make sense. This is the crucial turning point. One of two things will happen in this time. The victim will realize the relationship is lacking honesty and they will leave the relationship, or in a blind state of love, the victim will hope that there is somehow a reasonable reason for the behaviour of the other and they will stay.

Emotional stress will begin to mount in the victim at this time. A chronic liar can only come up with so many plausible excuses for whatever it is that they are hiding. The victim will begin the stage of wondering if they are seeing things correctly. How can you be sure? The answer is simple. If the other person in the relationship is consistently telling you things that simply do not make sense, this is a sign you are in this phase. Life is not perfect, it is normal for all of us to have "off" days, perhaps days in which strange events occur. However, it is improbable and inconceivable if you are being told illogical things on a reoccurring basis. If the other person has seemingly bizarre excuses for their behaviour and this has become the norm, it is not normal.

Most reasonable people do not repeatedly question others. If you find yourself having to ask many questions in an attempt to understand the "story" being told to you, it is not normal. If the words said to you make no logical sense, if it seems very apparent that they are lying but each time you question them, they create a new excuse and it is a continuous snowball, it is a clear sign that the other is not able to have an honest conversation. Normal, everyday conversations with a loved one should be stress-free. Normal conversations should not leave you bewildered. If one does not back away from the relationship at this point and continues to stay despite the signs of being lied too, it is at this point that the strong manipulation can occur.

If the relationship has made it this far, the victim of the lies has almost certainly made it clear that they are not happy with

Escaping the Power of Lies

the reasoning of the liar. They have probably accused the other of lying, and perhaps even pleaded for the truth. If wanting the relationship to last, the victim may express the need for honesty and tell the other that they need this element for the relationship to continue. However, the key here is that the victim is still in the relationship. This is showing the liar that despite questioning, despite being under suspicion, their lies are ultimately acceptable.

How does the liar create the manipulation to keep the victim in the relationship? By reversing blame; one of the ultimate emotional games. When confronted with suspicion, the liar will attempt to "turn the tables". They will attempt to make the victim feel guilty for "even thinking such a thought". They may tell the victim that they are in shock from the accusation of lying. They may tell the victim they love them, and would never do such a horrible thing as to lie. The liar may even swear on everything good and holy, on deceased loved ones and on their eyesight; but it is all a lie. This manipulation is done in a final attempt to make the victim believe they are paranoid.

The victim may be told that they are overly jealousy or overly curious and need to correct that "flaw". The victim can manipulate to feel as if they somehow are the one to create friction and problems in the relationship; that their questioning is causing turmoil. If the manipulation is strong enough, the victim may even feel they are losing their sanity. They may question their own ability to make judgments. Everything the victim correctly interprets as wrong, their loved one sternly tells them is indeed correct. With everything seemingly turned upside-down, the victim will feel confused. If vulnerable and feeling the strong need for love, the victims may even find themselves apologizing for any accusations.

It is at this time, that one of two things will happen. The victim will stay persuaded into believing they are to blame or the victim will open their eyes to the unpleasant but realistic fact that they manipulated and lied to. As in most difficult times of a person's life, the correct road to take is the hardest road to take.

When you love another person, when you have invested a large amount of time, emotion, and your very being into the relationship, it is sometimes easier to give in and believe the liar's excuses. It is far easier to believe that somehow, despite all of the illogical and unreasonable behaviour displayed and sometimes the blatant lies you hear that by some means, you are mistaken. Finally admitting that the person you love has been betraying you is the beginning of finally taking the step to ending the relationship. To admit that the person you love has been manipulating you as if you were a puppet, can be emotionally shattering. It can also be freeing.

While taking in a deep breath, allow yourself to stand back a bit and the truth of the relationship may take on a different form. As a victim, in your heart you know the qualities you desire in a mate. You know that being the kind and caring person that you are that you deserve love, respect, kindness, and honesty. Despite how much you felt you were in love, or feel you still are in love, was this the person the one that you have been dreaming of? Or more fittingly, was this person not, but somehow you wished they would be?

Escaping the Power of Lies

You never hoped for a deceitful mate. You never longed for a relationship that led to misery. You never listed "liar" as a trait you were looking for in a person. You most probably entered the relationship with an open heart and an open mind. A scheming person took advantage of your trust and they betrayed you.

You can never gain back the weeks, months or years lost to this relationship. No one has the capability to redo the past. However, you can be strong enough to take away the power of lies from the other person. If you walk away, and they do not have you as a target, you have stripped them of their power. Their feeling of supremacy will be gone. All of the efforts of their lies will come to a crashing halt. All of the time that they invested was in vain. They will be left alone to face the burden of their immoral ways. You will walk away knowing you will never have that burden on your shoulders.

Debunking the Common Myths about Liars

Our brains are geared to respond to external threats. These threats could be anything from someone pointing a gun at you, to lying about an extramarital affair. In both examples, you perceive a threat and your body prepares you to either run away or fight. In both situations, you have something to lose and your body will physically respond to the threat. The examination is based on psychological theories and physiological changes that occur when a person "tells a lie." Without going into a historical background, the foundation of the polygraph (lie detection, truth verifier) is based on the psychological theory of "fight or flight." What about nonverbal clues to lying? I recently discussed non-verbal clues of lying with a polygraph examiner. I have great respect for this individual, but in the end, we agreed to disagree on several issues. Let me provide you a few points from our discussion. Bear in mind that some of the following information is based on psychological/sociology studies and/or personal experience.

People who lie will not look you in the eye. Culturally, Latin and Asian nationals find it rude to stare at someone. In conversation, many will look around, occasionally make eye contact, but find it disrespectful to continuously "look you in the eye." Looking at someone in the eye as a means to firmly communicate and ensure they are receiving your message is part of the North American/European cultural. "I can't trust you if you don't look me in the eye." Remember that this isn't the case in all cultures.

People who lie, pause before answering a question since they are trying to come up with a believable lie. Actually, many people pause before answering a question. The reasons vary from trying to understand the question, to actually translating the question from one language to another. Pausing before answering may be a habit, a translation process or a method of actually trying to understand a complex question.

People who lie lower their tone/voice. Many Asian nationals will speak in a low tone when they first meet an individual from another country/culture It's a way to assess the individual and situation. It's a non-threatening mechanism that is used to communicate without appearing rude.

People who lie will ask you to repeat the question: it's possible an individual is attempting to provide you with a plausible lie, but what if the individual is just trying to understand the question or its meaning. A hearing impaired individual may need you to repeat the question to ensure they have heard correctly.

Application in Relationships: 10 Signs That She is Lying to You

Have you ever had the sinking feeling that your girlfriend is lying to you? Whether she is lying about whether or not she is being faithful, where she spent last week's paycheck or about whether or not you are the best lover she has ever had, there are a few telltale signs that you can watch for that will tell you if she is lying. While you probably cannot be 100% certain, these 10 signs can serve as good indicators of how truthful she is being.

Sign #1: Swallowing

You probably catch yourself frequently focusing on that luscious mouth of hers, so why not focus your attention on whether or not that mouth is telling a lie? Nearly everyone experiences a certain level of stress when he or she is lying, which causes constriction in the esophageal muscles. Since these muscles are used for swallowing, your lying girl may frequently swallow while she is laying a load of bull on your shoulders.

Sign #2: Licking Those Lips

While your girl may occasionally lick her lips seductively in order to get your motor running, licking her lips may also be a sign of telling a fib. This is because another side effect of stress is decreased saliva production, which means she may be suddenly left with a case of dry mouth when she tries feeding you a line. She might also clench her jaw or tighten her lips while talking to you.

Sign #3: Answering Questions with Questions

In an effort to stall or to avoid lying to you outright, she may start answering your question with another question. Don't let her get away with this tactic or allow her to stall - push for answers and don't get sidetracked by her questions.

Sign #4: Selective Memory

Another way to avoid telling an outright lie is to suddenly "forget" certain details. Again, pressing her for answers and asking for details will help you find out whether she is telling the truth or spinning a tale. Make certain to remember the details she shares, because she will likely contradict her own story if she is telling a lie.

Sign #5: Changes in Skin Tone

Many women also experience a change of skin tone when lying, which may be characterized by either getting suddenly flush or pale.

Sign #6: Voice Changes

Unless she is a pre-pubescent boy, your girl's voice shouldn't be cracking or changing pitch as she tells you her story. If her vocal tone changes or if her talking speed falters or speeds up, she is probably trying to think of the next part of her story or

Application in Relationships: 10 Signs That She is Lying to You

her nerves have gone into overdrive and she is having difficulty maintaining her normal breathing patterns.

Sign #7: Hiding Her Hands

Hands are more expressive than you may realize, which is exactly why she will subconsciously want to hide them from you. Therefore, if she is lying to you, she will likely keep her hands behind her back or under her armpits. If she thought through her story beforehand, however, she may keep her hands exposed but they will be resting in an unnatural position - such as resting flat on top of a table or hanging down by her side.

Sign #8: Pupil Dilation

No matter how skilled she is at telling a lie, the one thing she won't be able to control is pupil dilation. When you are under duress and your nerves kick in, your pupils will begin to dilate. If she has something to hide, she will likely get quite nervous as she tells you her story and her pupils will begin to spread with every word she utters.

Sign #9: Eye Movement

In a subconscious effort to prevent you from noticing her dilated pupils and because her guilty conscience makes it difficult for her to look you in the eye, she will likely begin to dart her eyes from side to side. She may also start blinking more than usual or possibly even lower her head completely so she doesn't have to face you.

Sign #10: Playing with Herself

Before you get excited, playing with herself doesn't mean what you think. Rather, she may start to fiddle with something in her hand in an effort to dispel her nervous energy. Or, she may begin rubbing or otherwise touching her own arms.

It is important to note that a woman displaying just one of these signs isn't necessarily lying. Obviously, there can be other reasons for experiencing dry mouth or for expressing other signs from this list. In addition, your girl may show some other signs that aren't on this list. So, pay close attention to her actions and try to get to know what is normal for her and what she does when you know she is lying. Still, if your girl is exhibiting three or more of these signs, chances are pretty good that you have a liar on your hands.

Application to Personal Life

How to Tell If You Are Being Lied To - Here Are the Earth Shattering Tricks You Can't Afford to Miss

It's a known fact that majority of human beings out there tend to lie on a regular basis. You see some lies can be forgiven but there are some lies which can cause a lifelong damage that are hard to deal with. This is the major reason why you must know how to catch such lies before it happens to you. Read on to discover some of the most mind blowing ways to catch a lie...

He/she would be anxious- This will be a very common sign if the person you are talking to you is lying to you. He/she would find it extremely hard to control his/her anxious feelings and this would be very obvious from the person's body language. And the fact of the matter is that they would act anxious only when asked a specific question, which is a clear sign that you are being lied to.

They will try to take extra time and will speak slowly- When a person is trying to lie to you, he/she would take extra time to make up something to escape your question and would either take some time before answering or would just speak very slow. You see, obviously if the person is stating facts, it shouldn't take him/her much time to actually answer you.

How To Read People And Spot A Liar

Taking extra time is a clear indication that he/she is trying to make something up.

Trying to avoid the subject- This is a very common thing a lot of liars do on a regular basis. They are masters at the art of sidetracking and changing the subject. Always try to be on the point and don't let the other person escape your question by changing the subject. Stick to the question until the time you get a clear cut answer.

Indicative Body Language

The gestures and bodily actions a person makes are indicative signs of lying. You will know that a person is deceiving you when his/her physical expression is stiff and limited. The person moves his/her arm infrequently. If ever the hands or legs move, it will be toward the person's body so he/she takes up less space. The lying individual will also avoid eye contact with you. Hands will also be touching the face, mouth, and throat. The person will also be expected to scratch or touch behind his/her ear.

Emotional Gestures

There are also emotional signs that a person is lying. Compared to when he/she is speaking to you honestly or in the usual manner, his/her emotional display will be delayed, will stay rather longer than usual or will suddenly stop. The timing of expression and making gestures are also off. For instance, if you gave that person a gift; ideally, he/she would smile and say thanks at the same time. You will know he/she is lying if the person first says thanks and then smiles afterward. Also, the emotions expressed by the words enunciated are contradicted. You know there is deception when the person says 'I like you' and yet, he/she is not even smiling. Fake emotions can also be made such as moving only the mouth, rather than involving the whole face to express feelings or emotions.

Showing Reactions

A person is guilty of lying when he/she is defensive. You can observe signs of discomfort from the liar when he/she speaks to you. As much as possible, that person would avoid making interactions or conversations with you. He/she will also unconsciously leave something between you and him/her as a form of block or obstruction to hide something.

Verbal Context

You can catch a liar from the context of the words spoken. If you ask a question, he or she will use the same exact words from your question to give an answer. Contractions of words will also be used by a liar. The lying person will also not make direct statements in order to avoid making lies. He/she will simply make implied answers and not actually deny something.

A guilty liar also speaks further than usual. He/she will mention redundant details in order to convince you. A liar will not remain comfortable staying silent or pausing from talking. You can also tell there is deception if the speaker enunciates words in a garbled manner. The person may speak rather softly, so that you will not clearly understand what is being said. There will also be some grammar or syntax errors in his/her statements. His/her sentences may be muddled and unclear.

The liar will also attempt to change the topic of conversation so your attention will be directed to other things. To avoid a subject, the liar will also use sarcasm or humor to comment or provide answers.

How to Tell if Someone is Lying in a Job Interview in Less Than One Minute

Today's labour market remains tough. When the market is competitive, the likelihood that there will be several candidates after a given job is high, so it is important to be able to differentiate individuals and spot the liars from the first minute to quickly get the best candidate before the other competitors.

Research shows that our ability to detect when someone is lying is just as good as an estimate or a guess. Perhaps, this is why lies get past us so often because our guess is that the person is not lying.

For most people, the act of lying elicits several reactions because it takes the brain some time to pause and not tell the truth.

Some of these reactions include an increased stress response (think Brian Williams), a stance of defiance and dominance (think Lance Armstrong), and a covering of true emotions, otherwise known as the truth (think Anthony Weiner).

Wouldn't it be great to know when you are being lied to? Or better yet, that you could get a heads-up before someone starts lying to you?

How To Read People And Spot A Liar

Lying is no more evident in public life as it is in everyday job interviews. While we may not be able to immediately detect if someone is lying, there are signs we can look for.

The key is to put our eyes and our ears into play to differentiate fiction from reality.

Baseline

When detectives are interrogating a suspect, they start with a set of non-threatening questions and observe the suspect's baseline behavior when answering. Then, they move to a difficult set of questions and observe changes in behavior that are indicative of deception.

For those in human resources management, this could look something like this:

Where did you grow up?

What are your favorite hobbies?

What are your strengths?

Simple enough. No reason to lie.

Next, the manager could ask questions like:

What would your last employer say about you?

What is the reason you didn't finish college?

What are your weaknesses?

How to Tell if Someone is Lying in a Job Interview in Less Than One Minute

A little bit more difficult and a little bit more of a reason to lie especially if their resume doesn't match up.

In the first set of questions, the potential employee will more than likely tell the truth. Then comes the hard part.

Do they pause, avoid eye contact, blink too much, move their feet, touch their face, or act like their thinking with the latter set of questions?

Breaking Eye Contact

Most people know that lying is wrong. When a liar is lying, s/he will break eye contact to reduce the guilt.

Holding eye contact can be overwhelming for a liar. Lying takes more energy than telling the truth because our brain has to pause and think about a lie to tell.

Conflicting Gestures

Let's say Jack is interviewing for the chief financial officer position of your company. You ask him if he has ever gone bankrupt. He gives you an affirmative "no" while at the same time shaking his head "yes."

Words may be lies, but the internal reactions within the body and brain force our gestures to be more truthful.

Duping Delight

Dr. Paul Eckman coined the phrase "duping delight" to refer to the glee that some people get when they feel they are being successful in manipulating someone else. Lying is a form of manipulation.

How To Read People And Spot A Liar

With a lie, you may see a micro-expression called duping delight which is a smile that comes across one's face when they feel they are getting away with something (think O.J. Simpson). When you feel someone is lying, look for a slightly suppressed smile.

Overcompensating Language

If you ask a question and the interviewee replies with a short story, then you are in for a few lies. Using too many words can be a sign that the person is hiding something.

Liars are good at trying to come across as truthful. It is their attempt that gives them away.

Turn Away, Turn Back

Following an answer or response that is less than truthful, liars will look away from you or pretend to be looking for something in a stack of papers or on there phone before returning the glance.

This is a tactic to see if you believe the lie and will move on to the next topic, or if you doubt the lie and will rephrase the question.

The One Dead Giveaway Almost Every Liar Makes When Telling a Story

Liars always look to the left, several friends say; liars always cover their mouths, says a man sitting next to me on a plane. Beliefs about how lying looks are plentiful and often contradictory: depending on whom you choose to believe, liars can be detected because they fidget a lot, hold very still, cross their legs, cross their arms, look up, look down, make eye contact or fail to make eye contact.

So, without further ado, here are 8 habits shared by Lying Larry's and Fibbing Franny's around the world.

1. 1. Averted gaze: It's not normal to expect someone to maintain full eye contact for the entirety of a conversation...unless they have some sort of disorder, and that's another story in and of itself. However, if you notice any difference in the amount of eye contact the suspected liar is making, that could be a clue that they're not telling the truth. In fact, even the direction of the gaze makes a difference when trying to figure out someone's intentions. It has been noted that when trying to recall a fact, most people will avert their eyes upwards and to the right. A person who is trying to come up with a lie, however, will usually look down.

2. 2. Too much eye contact: Just as a liar may avert his or her gaze to keep someone from looking into their eyes (it's been long said that you can see the truth in someone's eyes, therefore liars may try to avoid this result by looking away altogether), someone trying to cover up a lie may also make too much eye contact. This comes as a result of a reverse train of thought by the person in question. More experienced frauds may know that people are expecting them not to make eye contact and therefore counteract this by making prolonged eye contact, to the point of abnormality.

3. 3. Stuttering: Telling a lie, especially a more in-depth one, takes a lot of effort on the fibber's part. So much effort, in fact, that in the process of telling it, people tend to get tripped up. Think about it– if there's something big at stake, it takes enough effort to remember and relay an actual string of events. Liars charge themselves with the duty of not only coming up with a fake string of events, but also coming up with it on the spot as well as double-checking every word they say seconds before they say it, meanwhile paying strict attention to every word they say for fear that they'll be asked to repeat the same story later. Makes you almost feel sorry for them doesn't it? No!

4. 4. Sweating: It's a natural nervous reaction. Most people sweat or get sticky palms when speaking in public, making an important decision, waiting on significant results, etc. But if someone is sweating during an everyday situation, that could be a tip-off that they fear getting caught in their lie.

The One Dead Giveaway Almost Every Liar Makes When Telling a Story

5. 5. Abnormal expressions: As in the case of liars making too much eye contact, they may also go too far when it comes to showing they are at ease to throw you off. If someone holds a facial expression for too long, such as a smile, or other expressions/gestures, take that into consideration.

6. 6. Fidgeting: This may be a person's way of diverting your attention, therefore breaking your concentration on the facts of the story they're telling you. It may also be an uncontrollable nervous habit. Whether someone fidgets with an outside object or takes up a nervous habit such as tapping their feet or twirling their hair, these are all signs that your culprit may not be fully at ease and in the midst of spinning a tall tale.

7. 7. Changes in pace: Beyond the obvious stuttering through sentences, more experienced liars might try to disguise this dead giveaway by pausing excessively. You can watch for this by noticing where in the sentence or story the person pauses. If it's right before an important detail, or maybe before a detail they have relayed to you previously, this could be a sign that they are trying to straighten up their story in their head before it comes out of their mouth. Also, if the person pauses at irregular times such as the middle of a sentence (in the absence of a transition), they could be trying to let their voice catch up with their mind.

8. 8. Changes in tone of voice: When someone is spinning a story, they are usually concentrating too hard on coming up with the details for their body to focus on what it is normally able to focus on. This may cause a

55

person's voice to crack, which is almost a dead giveaway of a lie being told

For the most part, pegging the aforementioned signs as a tip-off of a lie comes down to knowing the person in question. On any given day, any given person could show any of these signs, while also remaining perfectly innocent. But if you know someone's normal tendencies, it becomes that much easier to peg these signals for what they really are, therefore catching their insincere act and taking proper actions.

Find Out if Anyone is on Drugs in Less Than Three Minutes

If you are an employer, an employee, a teacher, a student, a parent or a friend who has an interest in maintaining a safe environment (and who doesn't want that?) then you should know the tell-tale signs and symptoms of someone who is under the influence of drugs. Eight percent of full-time employed adults and 10% of part-time employed adults had substance abuse issues, according to the 2011 National Survey on Drug Use and Health. Don't let these small percentages fool you; they represent thousands and thousands of people, some of whom you might work with or see everyday!

Don't let a suspicion of drug abuse go by uninvestigated. Look for changes in the person's appearance and personality, and disruptions in their usual routine. The following signs may help you determine whether someone close to you is abusing drugs.

Physical Signs

There are several signs, both physical and behavioral, to look out for when investigating drug abuse. Each drug manifests differently in the body, but the following are some general indications that a person might be using drugs:

Keeping irregular hours, loss of sleep

Changes in eating habits

Red, watery eyes; pupils unusually large or small

Extreme hyperactivity; excessive talkativeness

Slow or staggering walk

Poor physical coordination

Tremors in the hands, feet, or head

Worsening hygiene or physical health

Frequent twisting of the jaw

Runny nose

Hacking cough

Blushing, pale or puffy face

Behavioral Signs

Drugs interfere with passageways in the brain, which can cause profound changes in moods and emotions. The following behavioral changes may indicate drug abuse:

Damaged relationships

Asking for money

Change in overall attitude

Find Out if Anyone is on Drugs in Less Than Three Minutes

Drop in performance at work and school

Chronic dishonesty

Inattentiveness; forgetfulness

Loss of motivation, energy, and self-esteem

Secretiveness, unusual demand for privacy

Change of wardrobe

Sudden oversensitivity; temper tantrums and Loss of interest in friends and family

Find Out Who's Stealing and Whom You Can Trust

Carefully document each instance of theft. Your biggest friend when it comes to catching thieves in your workforce is information. As soon as you notice that a theft has occurred, make a major effort to gather information that can help you pinpoint when, where, and, if possible, around whom the theft took place.

Data you may want to record and/or search your records for can include:

The exact time and date of when the cash or merchandise was first noticed missing

Starting and final totals for each register or point of sale (for when cash is being stolen)

Inventory counts and sales reports (for when goods are being stolen)

Names of employees working at the time the theft may have taken place

If possible, records of access card swipes, etc.

Employee expense reports

Records of equipment checkout

If you don't have this information, start recording it once you suspect a theft. This alone may be enough to discourage further theft, but if it doesn't, you'll be better prepared to catch thieving employees in the future.

Look for inconsistencies in your records. Narrow your search down by checking your records for instances where "the numbers don't add up." In other words, look for spots where money or goods appear to go missing. The better your record-keeping, the more likely you'll be able to find concrete evidence of theft.

For example, let's say that, when examining your inventory records, you notice that your records for one day show that you had 20 expensive smartphones in stock at the start of the day and that you had 10 in stock at the end of the day, but you only have records of nine being sold. This is a definite red flag and cause for future investigation.

Pay extra attention to special register functions. Employees that steal cash from their register at work often use a set of related tactics to cover their tracks. These basically involve inputting certain functions into the cash register incorrectly, then using the opportunity to pocket some cash. For example, a dishonest employee may use a register's "no sale" function to steal — when a customer hands over cash for her purchase, the employee may input the "no sale" command (which opens the register), pay the customer their change, and pocket a bill from the now-open register. The customer is unlikely to notice, and no sale is recorded.

Register functions that you may want to monitor closely include:

No sale

Refund

o sale items

Reports or print-outs (dishonest employees may pocket money paid while the register system is undergoing a report)

O'Dell Restaurant Consulting offers a comprehensive guide to common employee theft tactics, some of which take advantage of these special functions, here. While the focus is restaurant-centered, many of the tactics discussed are applicable to other fields like retail as well.

If cash is being stolen, instate a register-counting system. One common way to fight register theft is to use a system where each employee "checks out" a register cash box at the start of the shift and returns it at the end of the shift. When the cashbox is checked out, the money in it is counted, and when it's returned, the money is counted again and compared to a sales report. This system is relatively easy to put in place and, while it won't stop all forms of register theft, it will catch blatant thieves easily.

Using a standardized check-in/check-out spreadsheet can make this system much easier for both employees and their supervisors. Rows that you'll probably want to include on your spreadsheet include:

How To Read People And Spot A Liar

Starting cash

Cash sales

Credit card/check sales

Total sales

Ending cash

When possible, consult video surveillance data. If your business has a CCTV security system, examine the footage for evidence of stealing (especially if the cameras are pointed at locations where theft is likely to occur, like cash registers.) Use the information you've gathered to narrow down the time and place that the theft occurred to as small of range as possible, then watch closely for telltale signs of thievery, including:

An employee's hands passing bills from a register into her pockets

Bills going from a register to a tip jar

Strange habits around a cash register (e.g., some dishonest employees may subtly mark registers to remind themselves how much they've stolen so they can modify their reports accordingly)

Merchandise going into coats, purses, backpacks, and so on

"Good" merchandise going into the garbage

Unauthorized access to safes, cash boxes, etc.

After-hours access to the building

Hold one-on-one employee interviews for information. While a thieving employee is unlikely to admit to his crime if you confront him directly, honest coworkers may be willing to point you in the right direction. Consider calling your employees to your office for a personal, open discussion about the theft you've been experiencing. You can ask them if they know anything about employees who are stealing or if they're willing to help you work to stop this problematic behavior. You can also take the opportunity to remind your employees about your business's policies regarding theft.

When you conduct interviews, make sure that your interviews are done one-on-one behind closed doors. Your employees are most likely to be honest when they don't have to fear running afoul of other employees.

You'll also probably want to interview as much of your workforce as you can (every employee, if possible.) This gives your employees plausible deniability — in other words, if their information leads to a firing, it will be harder for the employee who gets fired to figure out who outed him.

Consider hiring an outside investigator for an internal audit. It's worth mentioning that owners and supervisors don't necessarily have to fight workplace theft on their own. A huge variety of independent consultants and investigation firms specializing in company security and theft prevention are available for help. While the cost of hiring this sort of outside help may not make it worth it for small incidents of theft, these third-party solutions can be indispensable for larger problems.

This sort of help can also be especially useful when the theft is occurring at the bookkeeping level of a business. Dishonest bookkeepers can potentially bilk relatively large amounts of money from a company's payrolls without calling attention to themselves, making an objective outside auditor highly useful.

Especially in tough times, people may be less trustworthy than we'd like or expect.

So, how do you figure out whom and how much to trust?

Before trusting a person, try to determine how often he or she is correct. For example, read Yelp reviews of physicians, not so much to see whether patients like them, but how often the doctors correctly make a difficult diagnosis.

If you're thinking of trusting someone with money, assess how financially desperate or materialistic they may be. I'd be a bit dubious of someone who drives a Jaguar and wears a Rolex.

Most important, I'd want to see if a person acts justly even when it's inexpedient. That is especially key if the person has much to gain by acting against your interest and you're unlikely to detect it.

It's a double blow, to lose your hard-earned cash or property and to have such valuables taken by someone you know. Both aspects of the crime are rotten. The challenge, as the victim, is handling both forms of betrayal to keep the rot from taking hold.

It's a paradox to be sure, to cultivate trust even as you recognize that people violate it; or to accept that a crime was perpetrated against you without allowing it to recast your identity. The point is to move on from the event while learning from it, and to reclaim both your stuff and your confidence. It's not easy, and it often hurts like hell, but such is the work of healing.

Is The Wool Being Pulled Over Your Eyes in a Negotiation? Find Out

Negotiators often don't say everything they're thinking. Sometimes they hold back or distort information to avoid being exploited by the other party. Disclosing your "walk away" or "must have" conditions can frequently be a risky strategy – particularly with aggressive competing negotiators on the other side.

How many times have you been fooled by the other party claiming to have decision making authority, when in reality that wasn't the case? Or maybe they make commitments they have no intention of keeping?

So How Do You Spot This?

The truth is that people are not as good as they think they are in picking up on deception or outright lies. Studies have shown that many people's gut feelings about when people are lying are not much more reliable than tossing a coin. When you are under pressure this is even worse. In phone negotiations this is even more problematical because you have no opportunity to pick up the non-verbal clues or incongruities in others' behaviours.

Fortunately, those negotiators skilled in human observation- including psychologists, poker players, and actors-can teach us a number of strategies for distinguishing a lie from the truth.

1. Be completely aware of all behaviours

> Professor Paul Ekman has pioneered the study of what he calls "micro-expressions". These are small facial movements that are extremely difficult to detect. People assume that failure to make eye contact is a sign of lying in negotiations. Sometimes it is – but some people are just lacking in confidence or are shy – particularly in a high stress situation. Other studies have revealed that staring or eye-balling is used by many to conceal a lie, perhaps due to the popularly held belief that looking away shields a lie.

2. Listen, all the time

> The Verbal content of the conversation is frequently the best indicator of attempted deception. A few of the key behaviours are listed below:
>
> Uses your words – allows them to get the answer out fast without processing the information
>
> They won't stop talking – the nervousness means they continue to provide more and more information, or repeat themselves like a dog chasing its tail
>
> They aggressively stonewall in an attempt to limit challenges
>
> They don't answer the question directly

Is The Wool Being Pulled Over Your Eyes in a Negotiation? Find Out

The reactions are disproportionate to the questions

The 3rd party view may be missing from the story

Answer your questions but don't ask any

Immediate relaxation when subject is changed

Not indignant or excessively indignant when accused

Humour or sarcasm

Answers a negotiation question with a question

Suddenly starts stammering, develops a nervous tick or twitch, or starts blinking excessively

Expresses extreme displeasure at another – on your team or their own

3. Look for anomalies

Some people are highly attuned to picking up the non-verbal cues that give away lies. One of the best ways for a layman to pick up half truths is to watch for inconsistencies or anomalies. Ask yourself: was their behaviour consistent? So when considering the above list of behaviours in your negotiations, ensure that you compare their suspicious behaviour to how they behave normally to spot a lie. To do this you need to be tuned into their normal behaviour – which can be a challenge if you're negotiating with a team or haven't known the other party for very long. All the more reason to invest in the relationship first and not talk business too soon.

So if they normally listen attentively, answer your question promptly, use the language you've used in your question, and blink briefly before answering – be on alert if they pause for longer before answering, their eyes focus on a member of their team instead of just blinking, they neglect to use the language you've used in your question, and they lean back unconcerned instead of listening to your response. They may not be lying, the onus however is on you to probe further to uncover the reason for their behaviour change.

4. Ask the right questions

In negotiation, the question "Is that really your best offer?" almost always elicits a "Yes." No one is going to say, "Well, actually, it isn't. I was just hoping you'd think so." A better strategy is to give the other party an out. If someone says, "Take it or leave it." One option is to simply treat the statement as untrue for the moment, discuss further and make a counter-proposal. The truth of an ultimatum is tested by whether the person making it is willing to consider alternatives. It's up to you to float them.

How to Get Someone to Confess When You Have No Leverage Whatsoever

Lies are inevitable, but getting duped isn't. When you're in the presence of a liar, you can often uncover the truth by paying attention to very specific nonverbal cues. You just need to ask the right questions and observe their body language to catch them in the act.

When someone's lying, they will probably give off a few nonverbal cues that suggest something is "off," but they don't prove that someone's lying to you.

Use Nonverbal Cues to Investigate Possible Lies

While nonverbal cues won't prove that someone's lying, they can direct your investigation by highlighting the important clues. Pamela Meyer, author of the book Liespotting and CEO of deception training company Calibrate, says you should start off an interview by asking your suspect easy, stress-free questions. From there, you can get a "baseline" of their body language when they aren't under any pressure. Then, when you start asking more pointed questions about the lie you're investigating, you can pick out which words make them more anxious or distressed.

Of course, not all cases are so simple. If you really need the detailed truth, you may have to ask quite a few questions before you have enough evidence to figure it out. In other cases, if you ask the right questions, the person will realize you're onto them and confess. Whatever you do, though, Meyer says putting pressure on them isn't the answer

In general, a truthful person will have less of a problem telling their story backwards (though it may still be a tad difficult). Navarro agrees that pressure is a bad strategy, noting that "if you use any kind of pressure on somebody, what you're going to get is compliance. Compliance gets you a limited amount of information." Cooperation, on the other hand—building up that rapport and that trust—will have them giving you much more.

The best way to do this is to signal through your words and actions that your world is an honest one, that you act with integrity. Also why look down your nose at someone who just committed a moral act you never would? What's the point? Try hard to be focused on facts and not on judgement of others. Often people will feel more freedom to be honest when they do not feel that their questioner is being morally dismissive or superior. As well, try to understand one's motivation for doing whatever they are lying about, and provide a no-judgements attitude when discussing what motivated them, And never ask "why did you do it?" Asking "why" directly always puts someone on the defensive. Instead suggest several different reasons one might have for committing whatever act is under discussion and let your subject choose what to share with you.

In short: The less accusatory of a tone you take, the more likely you'll get cooperation from your subject. Know what questions you need to ask, look for the right cues, and do some digging yourself. When you've uncovered enough evidence, you'll either have a strong case for the truth or they'll confess to you willingly.

Meet one-to-one. Nobody confesses to a crowd. Bring food: people are more likely to open up when they're eating as they associate food with pleasure. Plus, it makes you likeable and makes others feel indebted to you.

Don't be accusatory. Instead, show empathy and sympathy, and be sincere. Talk slowly and quietly and start with a Direct Observation of Concern (DOC). For example: 'Thank you for agreeing to speak with me. I do appreciate it. The thing is, some of what you're saying isn't adding up, and I need you to help me understand what I'm missing.'

Don't ask questions; create a monologue. Imply that you already know what they've done, that you understand the pressures that led to their understandable mistake and if they can confess, then you can work together on fixing the problem. A guilty person just wants to be understood, because it allows them to feel they've been forgiven.

Cultivate short-term thinking. The moment the person starts thinking of the long-term consequences of their lie, they will clam up. So don't dwell on the potential consequences of the truth. Use statements like: 'It's a fixable problem' and help them to save face by saying things like: 'Good people sometimes do stupid things'.

Hold up your hand if they deny they are lying to indicate they need to stop talking. Use the person's first name and repeat your monologue, using phrases such as: 'We just need to figure out why this has happened and fix it'.

Do not accuse; use a presumptive question. Instead of saying: 'Did you take the money?', which gives your interviewee the message that you still don't know if it's true, assume it is true and ask: 'Where is the money now?'

How to Tell Anyone's True Intent in Any Situation by Asking Four Simple Questions

How exactly can we find these bad intentions in toxic people from the get-go? Some of them are extremely subtle with their intent and can be some of the most amazing liars in the world. But if you are able to pick up on these warning signs in a person, chances are you've caught them before they could even make a move on you.

1. Tirelessly Needy

> Toxic people will often engage in conversations with others only to talk about themselves. They will make it seem like they are very interested in what's going on in your personal life, but somehow always manage to flip the conversation back to themselves again.

> They will relentlessly shower you with how many things they need and all of the things that they want. This isn't just a general need or want, they will tell you exactly what they need from you or what they want you to do for them. Do not fall prey to this manipulation.

2. Silver Tongue

Toxic people have the tongue of a demon when they want to persuade someone into doing something they want. For some reason, they have this ability to spin words into a fabricated mess that seems almost too good to be true. They are some of the most amazing liars, always testing the people around them to see who is worthy of their time.

Do not listen to or let their persuasive words make you do something you really don't want to do. Listen to your own gut and remove yourself from any situation that makes you uncomfortable with that person. They are going to try and manipulate you further if you don't.

3. One Thing On Their Mind

There is only one thing on their mind and that's getting you to do their bidding. The only reason for them to do any of this to anyone is so they can achieve whatever goal they have planned for that interaction.

You will begin to notice that they talk about the same things over and over again in an attempt to sink the idea into your head that you should help them with whatever it is they are looking for. Do not oblige. Refuse to give them what they want even if they are a broken record. You can still say no, change the topic, or leave the situation entirely.

4. Have A Bad Feeling?

If a toxic person has just finished talking to you and you feel as if you're misunderstood, irritated, unsure, or just have an extremely bad feeling in general, then you have

How to Tell Anyone's True Intent in Any Situation by Asking Four Simple Questions

just witnessed what it's like to fall prey to someone with bad intentions.

These people leave you feeling as if you weren't even heard, like you were just talking to a wall the whole time, that somehow they pulled a fast one on you. Do not fall victim to these negative feelings; that is what they want you to feel deep inside. They feed off that energy and use it to their advantage.

5. Irregular Eye Contact and Body Language

Even though a liar may have a very hard time looking a person in the eye, they still do their best to demonstrate proper body language as well as eye contact. For them, this makes them seem like a "normal" human being with normal, good intentions.

This couldn't be further from the truth. If you begin to notice that they have these irregular movements about them, chances are they are going to want to take you for a ride. Do not let them, look them dead in the eyes, watch their hand movements to see if they cover their mouth or face. Sweating is a good indication, and so is constant blinking.

Who is a true ally and who is out to sabotage you

In this life, there are enemies and allies to your progress. The key to greatness is sorting out those enemies and allies so that you can spend more time and energy on the allies and ignore or avoid the enemies.

Now this may seem like an obvious thing...but anything that seems so obvious is something you might take for granted. Or something that might be more complicated than you think.

For example: with where I'm at in my career, a lot of people would be tempted to say I've "made it."

Personally, I believe in never peaking, so I don't usually think of myself as the guy who "made it." I think of myself as the guy who has many more mountains to climb. And honestly, this seems to be a pretty common attitude among super successful people. But for the sake of this argument, let's say I have made it.

Guess what: I'm still discovering new enemies and new allies in my life that I never knew I had!

So it's important for all of us, wherever we are in the journey, to think carefully about the enemies and allies in our lives.

Sabotage is Your Enemy

The first thing you have to realize about this process is that it's not about what you like or dislike.

In fact, a lot of the most dangerous enemies for an entrepreneur are the ones that seem comfortable or enjoyable at first glance.

Think of it this way: if some stranger were to walk up to you and tell you your idea sucks, that might get under your skin, but at least it's out in the open. You can pretty easily discount that guy's opinion and move on.

How to Tell Anyone's True Intent in Any Situation by Asking Four Simple Questions

But what if there's someone in your life who loves you (or says they do) and they tell you "not to aim too high"? What if they claim that they're "trying to keep you safe" and "protect you from disappointment"?

Or maybe that voice is in your own head...

Whoever is saying that, whether it's your best friend, your significant other, your family, or yourself, you need to sit down with them and have a serious talk.

Because the truth is, that voice of safety and comfort is an enemy to your progress.

Come on man, you're an entrepreneur! You're supposed to get your hands dirty! You're supposed to grind and grind and grind til you think you've run dry! You're supposed to fail, over and over again, until you get it right in a big way!

Taking the comfortable route, or the safest route, or even the most balanced route, is not going to put you in a position to make the big wins you need to be a true leader.

Regardless of the person's intentions, when someone tells you to take the "safe route" they are sabotaging you.

Now does that mean you have to cut them out of your life entirely? Let me put it this way: you are 100% in control of who you spend your time with, who you talk to, and you listen to.

Maybe letting go of certain people will liberate you. Maybe for others you just need to spend less time with them. Your call.

Besides, look at where that "stay safe" advice is coming from…I'm willing to bet that the people saying that have never experienced any huge successes in their careers.

Sure, they may have an "okay" job and "okay" money, and maybe they're doing great in other parts of their lives, but let's be real here: are any of them making 6, 7, or 8 figures?

BONUS

How to Use Hypnotic Suggestions Like a Pro in Only Minutes

That's just one measly little minute.

Barely enough time to boil the kettle, and certainly not long enough to boil an egg.

No matter what you're doing, 60 seconds is quick. Whatever the activity, it'll seem like you just got started and then it's over.

That short space of time is enough to accomplish some things, though. And one of those things is...

... to hypnotize someone.

Ironically, it'll take you much longer to read this book than to perform a full hypnotic procedure. Yes, it'll take practice, and yes, there are a lot of separate steps involved. But once you get the hang of it you'll be able to go through the whole process in a flash.

So what exactly does the 60 second hypnotist process involve?

There are 10 different parts to work through, although some of those parts are actually very short sentences. The whole thing starts with your intention. If you're a regular reader you'll recognize that as H+.

Here is a list of the 10 steps with an explanation of what they mean so you know exactly how to hypnotize someone in 60 seconds!

Ready?

1. H+ – Contact – Permission

   H+ refers to your intention to do your best for the person you're going to hypnotize. It means getting switched on so you're as positive and energetic as possible. With only 60 seconds to work in, you haven't got time to waste. So you need to jump right in with your mindset already on fire.

   To make the process successful in the given time, you need help. Some of that help comes in the form of encouraging your subject to go deeper into a trance as quickly as possible. One way of doing that is by touching them on the arm or shoulder. And that brings us directly to the third element in this stage.

   Before you start touching the other person on the arm or shoulder, you need to get their permission. It doesn't have to be in writing, but you have to get it nevertheless. As well as providing you with a simple but effective tool to deepen the trance, it's also the first step in breaking down any barriers they might have. If they give you permission to do that, they'll be willing to give you permission for other things as the induction progresses.

BONUS: How to Use Hypnotic Suggestions Like a Pro in Only Minutes

Wow! We're only at step 1, and there are already 3 things to remember. But don't worry. The point is that you'll be doing these 3 things simultaneously. And once you become familiar with the technique you'll do it almost instantly. Here's an example of how this first step might work in practice:

"From time-to-time I may want to touch you on the arm or shoulder as part of the work, is it OK with you if I do that?"

That's it. You've asked for permission to make contact. Just make sure you bring your H+ attitude to the ballgame and everything else should flow smoothly.

2. Induce Trance

The second step is where you quickly induce the trance. You don't need to make a song and dance about it – just go for it. It's really the simplest step of the bunch, so let's look at an example before we get to the explanation.

"Close your eyes and go into hypnosis."

You'll notice that this is in the form of an instruction. You're not asking them to go into hypnosis, you're telling them. We can assume that if they've given you permission to touch them that they're going to continue doing what you say. As luck would have it, that's human nature, which in this case is working in your favor.

At first glance it looks like a pretty innocuous statement. But there's something else going on. Notice the use of the word "and" in the sentence. If you haven't spotted it, this is one of those power words.

85

It's also a bridging word, linking two things together that might not necessarily belong together. In other words, there's no reason why closing your eyes should make you go into hypnosis. The one thing doesn't automatically follow the other. When you state it like this, however, the unconscious mind gets the message and is coaxed into following along.

3. Deepen The Trance

By now your subject should be well on their way to trance. This is the point where you want to deepen the trance. The deeper they go, the easier it becomes to bypass the conscious mind and get at the unconscious. Unless that happens, you won't be able to address whatever the issue is, so the whole procedure will be pointless.

If you can count backwards from 5 down to 1, this step is a piece of cake. Your goal is to encourage them to switch off and let the hypnotic process happen. And the way to do it is something like this:

"Now, I am going to count down from 5 to 1, and every count will bring you ten times deeper into trance. 5... 10 times deeper into trance. 4... ten times deeper. 3... 2... 1."

We're about a third of the way through already. The next steps include a couple of Boilerplates, sort of blueprints that can be used over and over from subject to subject without making any radical changes to them. Boilerplate 1 (BP1) covers steps 4, 5 and 6 as follows.

4. Sounds Around You

This is an important stage in the process, particularly when you're performing hypnosis outside, for a social occasion, or at any time when there's background noise. That could be anything from a ticking clock to a passing fire engine to people talking in a corridor or nearby room.

You're trying to achieve two things with this step: you want to use any sounds in the environment to your advantage, and you want to get your subject tuned in to your voice. You can't work with someone who's distracted, so your first priority is to make sure any background noise isn't an issue. You can do that by saying something like this:

"Now, the sounds around you simply allow you to go deeper into hypnosis."

That's the first part of the statement. You're instructing the subconscious mind to either ignore any background noise or to use it as a trance deepening tool. The second part builds on that, directing their focus where it's needed most:

"... and allow you to focus on my voice."

You'll notice the use of the word "and" again to link the two things together. This last piece of the instruction tells them that the most important thing is the sound of your voice, no matter what else they might happen to hear. The Boilerplate continues into step 5, where you quickly reinforce the idea that they must listen to you.

5. My Voice

At this stage in the process you're building up to the point where you can implant suggestions for change. Since your words are all you have to use, it's crucial that your subject listens to everything you say.

That's important because during hypnosis it's possible for them to drift off into a world of their own. And when that happens, they won't be paying any attention to you and might not be able to hear a word you say.

Your goal here is to make a suggestion so they keep listening to your voice regardless of anything else. Here's one way to do that:

"Now, as you experience this state of hypnosis, you will notice that my voice follows you wherever you go, which allows you to hear my voice, and the meaning behind my words."

You want them to be tuned in to your voice and everything you say. But you don't want your words to go in one ear and out the other. So that's why the final phrase instructs them to do more than simply listen – they also need to understand what you're saying. That guarantees that they'll be focusing on your voice and your words.

And that brings us to step 6, the last part of BP1.

6. Safety – Sanctuary

No-one is going to willingly let you do things to them under hypnosis unless they trust you. You need to make them feel safe in your care by providing a simple zone of sanctuary. It doesn't have to be complicated, and in fact, it can be the very chair they're sitting on.

This is vital for two reasons. First, it makes them feel secure. They know that whatever happens they'll be safe with the chair beneath them. Second, this feeling of security gives them the confidence to explore the hypnotic experience without fear or apprehension. You always want to keep the experience positive (H+), and giving them a sense of safety and sanctuary allows the process to unfold in a constructive and uninhibited way.

To provide safety and sanctuary, simply say something like this:

"Feel the chair beneath you, and know that you are safe."

That's all there is to it. The chair works as a physical anchor so they know that, wherever you take them, they've always got a solid base to return to.

Step 7 stands alone, coming smack bang in the middle of the two Boilerplates.

7. Suggestions – Change Work

This is the crux of the whole process, the reason for hypnotizing someone in the first place. Here you can make suggestions based on what your subject hopes to accomplish, which you would have discussed with them before you began the hypnosis. There are too many options to consider in the space of this book, of course.

However, if you wanted to test out some impromptu hypnosis, here's a sample hypnotic gift of what you might say. This is designed to help fellow hypnotists believe in themselves and their power to help other people:

"You know that you are alive, which means that you have an effect on this world, and that means you are learning so much more about hypnosis than you ever thought possible, because hypnosis is an amazing gift that you get to give to others to improve their lives."

This might be a powerful suggestion to use with a beginning hypnotist, or with someone who has doubts about their abilities. Again you'll notice the use of linguistic bridges or linking words (such as "and" and "because") to connect unrelated phrases together.

The next 3 steps form part of the second Boilerplate or BP2.

8. Re-induction

Once your subject is in a trance, you have the power to pass on a couple of amazing and priceless gifts. One is the ability to give their self-esteem a fast and effective boost. The other is the ability to enter a trance more quickly and enjoy their next hypnotic experience more fully.

That's what the re-induction step does. It plants a suggestion in the subject's unconscious mind so that going into a trance will be easier in the future. So that next time a trance is induced it will happy quicker and more effortlessly. And naturally that means their experience will be deeper and more meaningful.

BONUS: How to Use Hypnotic Suggestions Like a Pro in Only Minutes

By this time your subject should be deep in a trance, hanging on your every word, and all you need to do is say something similar to this:

"Now, you are in hypnosis, which means that the next time you choose to go into hypnosis, you will find it easier than ever before, and you will have the privilege of experiencing hypnosis even deeper than before."

9. Self-esteem

Wouldn't it be amazing if, as a hypnotist, you could help make the world a better place? Well, listen up, because you can. You can make your subjects feel better about themselves by boosting their self-esteem while they're in a trance state.

As you'll see shortly, it's actually very easy to do. So the question is, why wouldn't you do it? The whole procedure won't take more than 60 seconds from start to finish. If during that time you could increase someone's self-belief with just a few words, you'd be silly not to, right?

You're giving them a gift, as mentioned above, but you're also doing something else. You're using your skill in a constructive and positive way. You're incorporating H+ into your work, not just at the beginning, but all the way through. And that's pretty cool.

How can your words have such a dramatic effect? The reason is obvious. By this time you're actually communicating with your subject on an unconscious level. Tell their unconscious mind how amazing and wonderful they are, and it will believe it. It won't argue or try to analyze your words, because unlike the critical factor part of the conscious mind, it doesn't work that way.

Think of it as giving them a mental pat on the back, encouraging and motivating them at the same time.

10. Re-emerge – Good Work

This is the final step in the process where you bring your subject out of trance and back to normal consciousness.

Your aim here is to do 2 things: to help them safely return from the hypnotic trance, and to reinforce the experience. Some people will refuse to believe they've been hypnotized. Telling them how well they did confirms that they really were under hypnosis, which will also make any suggestions you made more effective.

This step is like the opposite to step 3 where you deepen the trance. To help them re-emerge from the trance, you should count from 1 up to 5. It's also a good idea to include a few positive words to give them a sense of accomplishment.

And there you have it. It took more than 60 seconds to get through it all, but it won't take any longer when you put it into practice.

Just read the bits of sample suggestions you'll find in each of the steps and you'll get the idea. Typed up on their own, they'd probably only fill about half a page or so. There really isn't very much to it at all.

BONUS: How to Use Hypnotic Suggestions Like a Pro in Only Minutes

Practice it on people you know in the same way that you might rehearse a speech. Get it down pat so you know exactly what's coming next and what you're going to say. Then, go out and use it.

While you're at it, why not give yourself a challenge? See how many people you can work your magic on in one minute or less. The more you do it, the easier and more natural it will become.

Conclusion

Being able to determine who is telling you the truth and who is telling lies, may be one of the best assets you ever acquire. It could save you from being duped into handing your money over to an unscrupulous person, or it could just be a way of finding out who is eating all your biscuits at work. Either way, use your new found skills wisely and get spotting who is lying to you today!

Printed in Great Britain
by Amazon